THE CLASSICAL GUITAR COLLECTION
LUDOVICO EINAUDI

Order No. AM1000890

ISBN: 978-1-84938-594-7

To acces audio visit:
www.halleonard.com/mylibrary

4950-9944-0984-7038

HAL•LEONARD®

Visit Hal Leonard Online at
www.halleonard.com

Contact us:
Hal Leonard
7777 West Bluemound Road
Milwaukee, WI 53213
Email: info@halleonard.com

In Europe, contact:
Hal Leonard Europe Limited
42 Wigmore Street
Marylebone, London, W1U 2RY
Email: info@halleonardeurope.com

In Australia, contact:
Hal Leonard Australia Pty. Ltd.
4 Lentara Court
Cheltenham, Victoria, 3192 Australia
Email: info@halleonard.com.au

The Italian-born composer/pianist, Ludovico Einaudi, is one of the major success stories of classical music at the beginning of the new millennium. His worldwide reputation has been based on phenomenal CD sales of several albums, most recently *Una Mattina*, *Divenire* and *Nightbook*, and sell-out live performances on frequent international tours.

Einaudi was born in Turin in 1955, studied first at the Conservatory in Milan and later with Luciano Berio. In the mid-1980s he began to establish his own personal idiom in a series of works, firstly for dance and multimedia and then for piano. The idiom for which Einaudi's mature work has become so popular is ambient, meditative and often introspective, drawing on minimalism, world music and contemporary pop. He has made a significant impact in the film world, most recently with a number of key tracks on *This is England* and the score for *The End is My Beginning*.

CALMO

MUSIC BY LUDOVICO EINAUDI

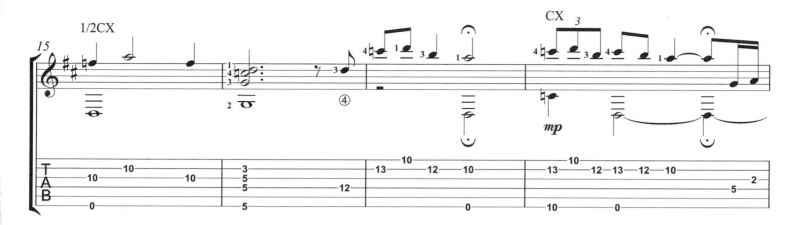

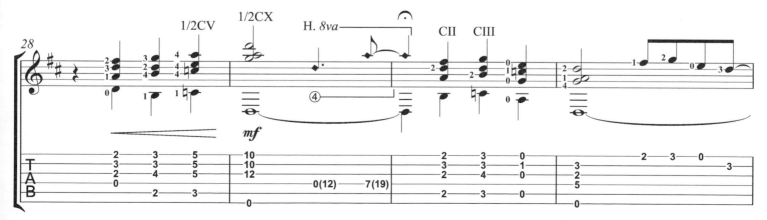

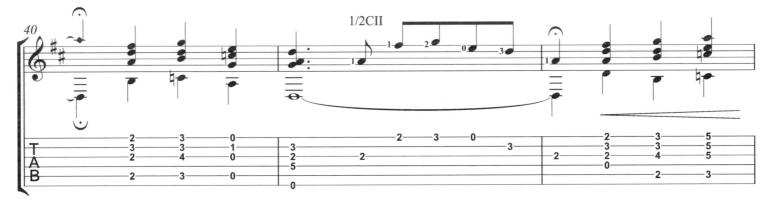

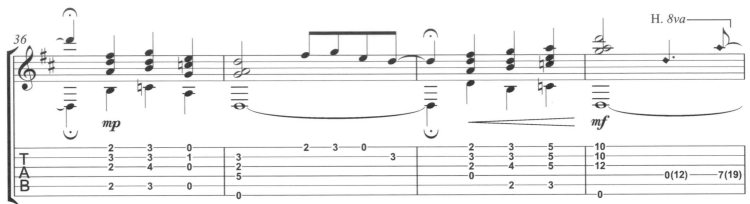

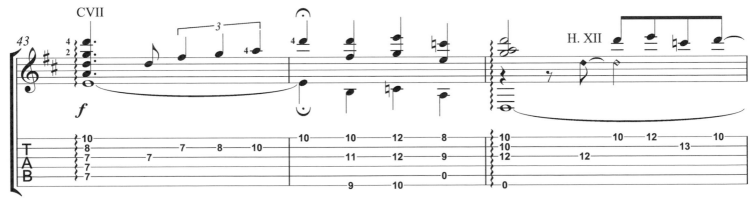

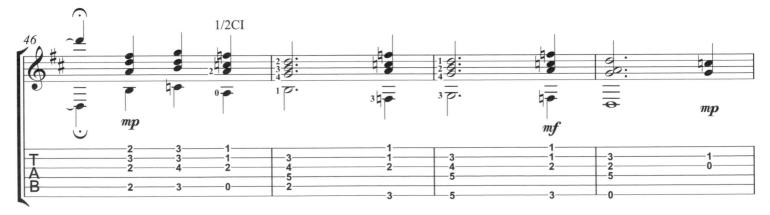

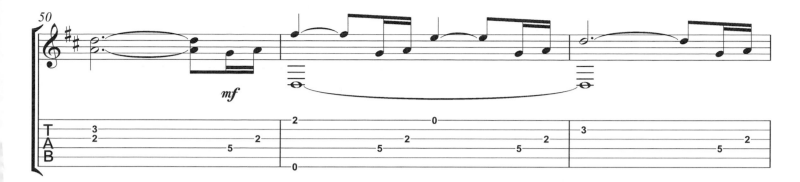

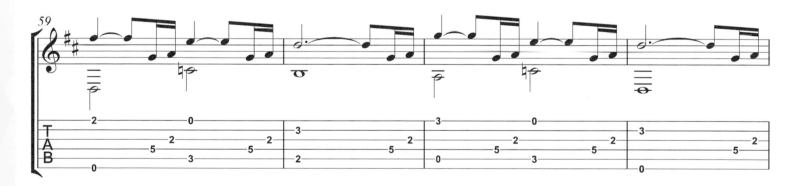

7

DIETRO CASA

MUSIC BY LUDOVICO EINAUDI

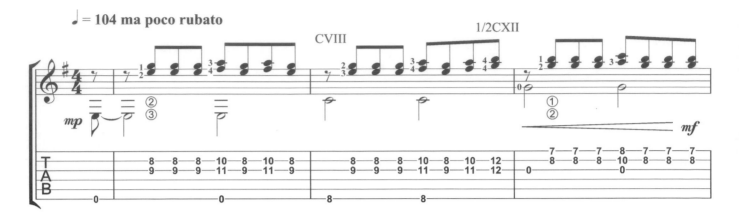

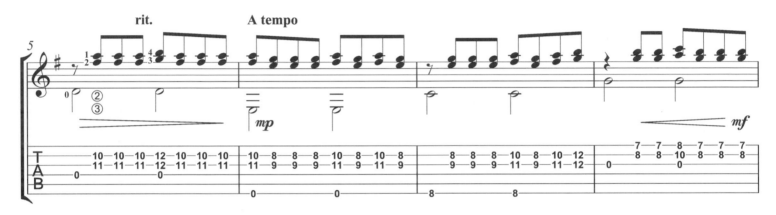

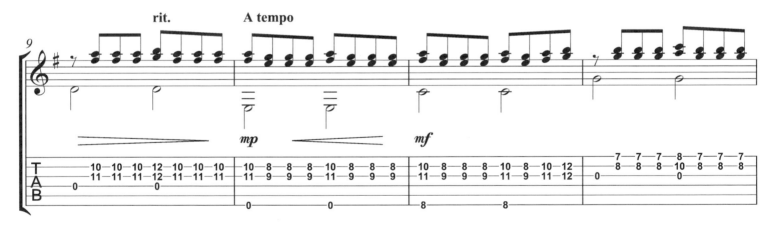

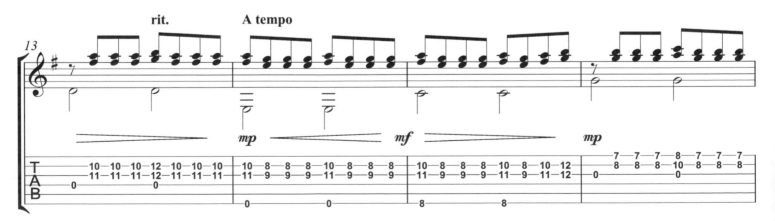

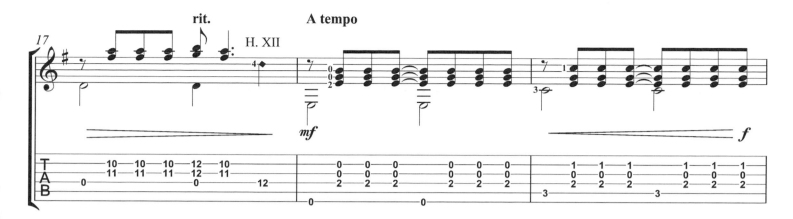

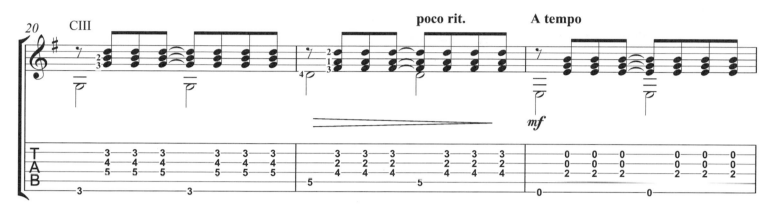

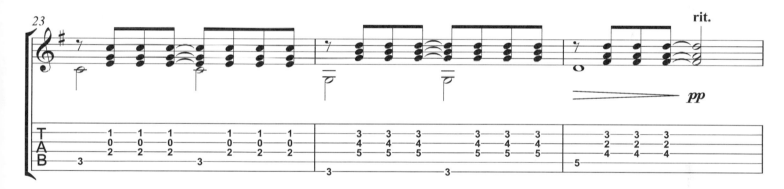

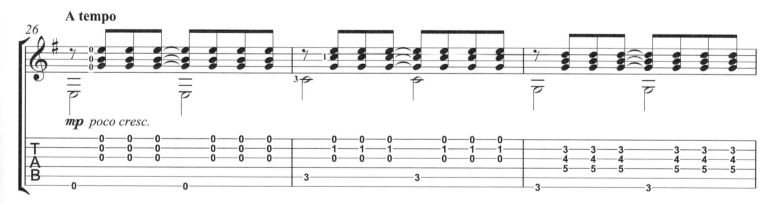

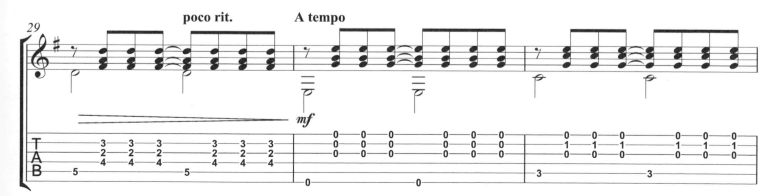

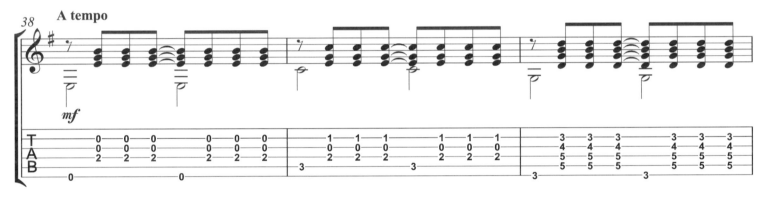

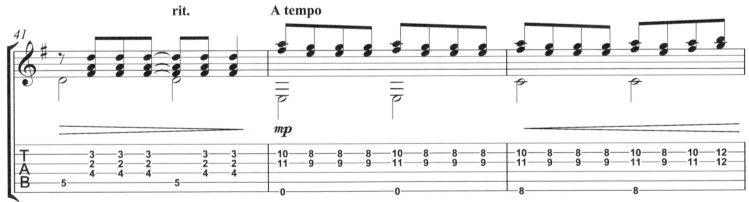

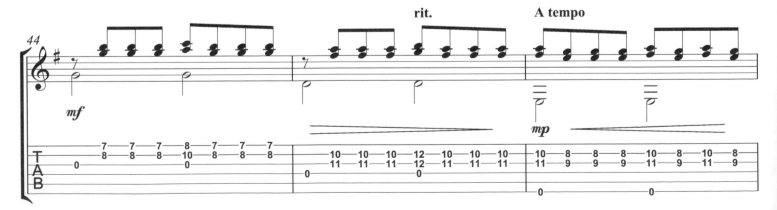

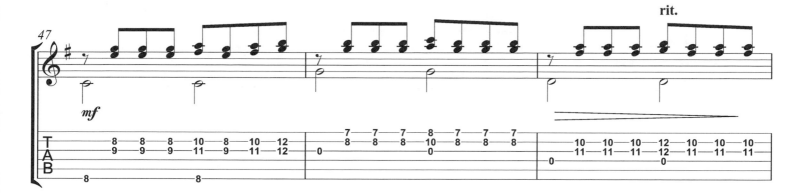

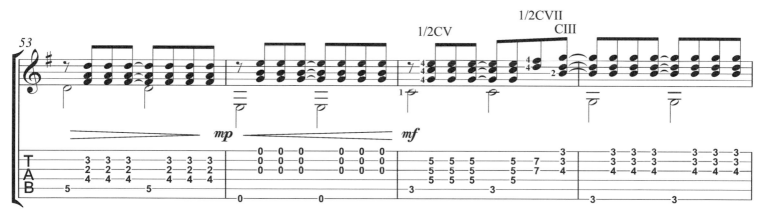

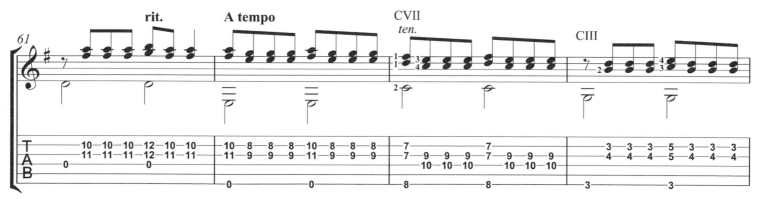

11

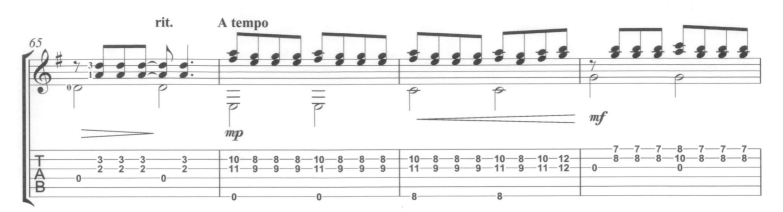

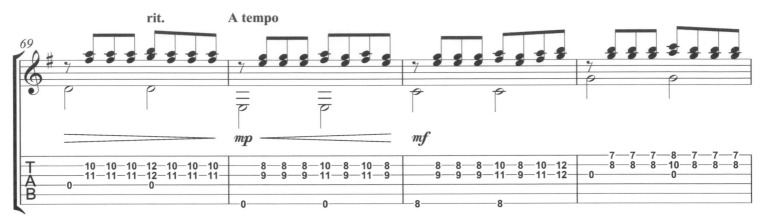

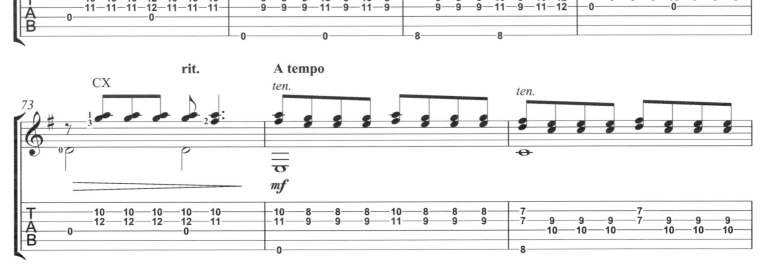

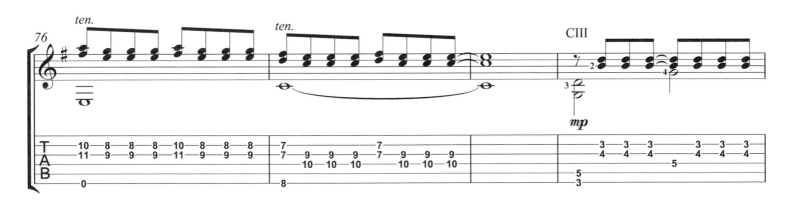

DIVENIRE

MUSIC BY LUDOVICO EINAUDI

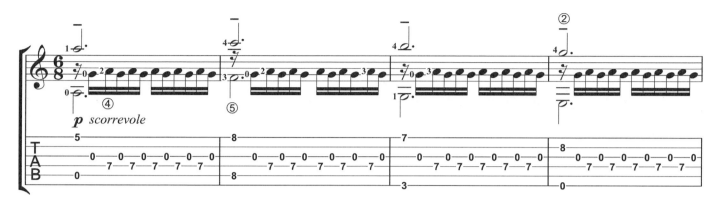

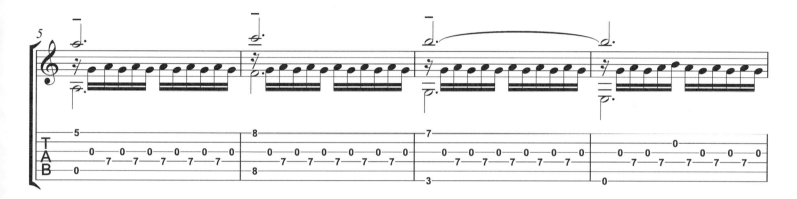

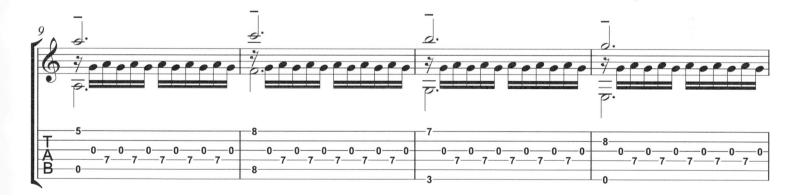

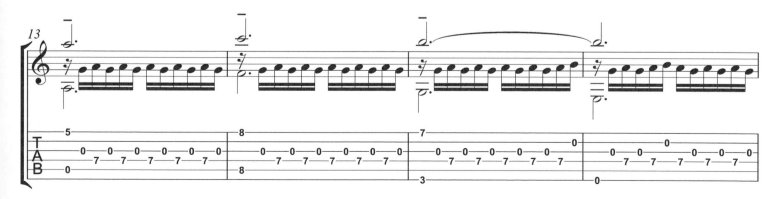

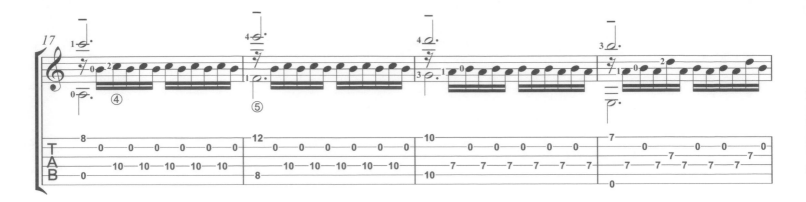

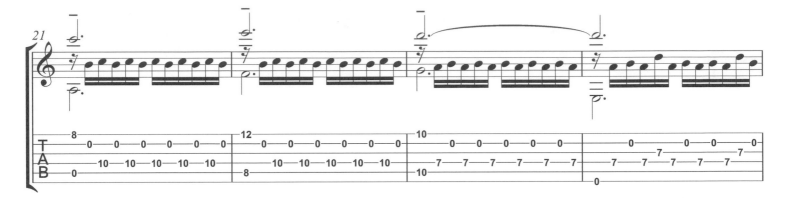

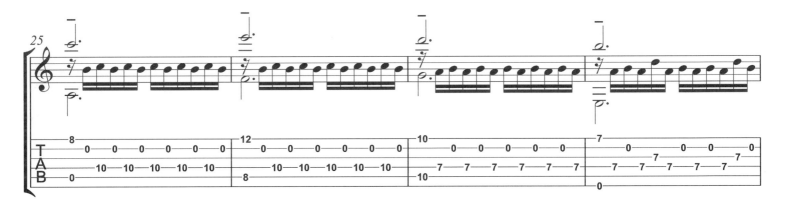

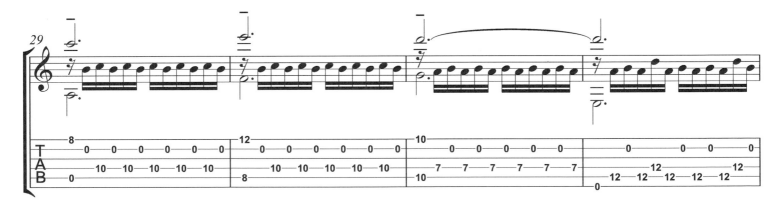

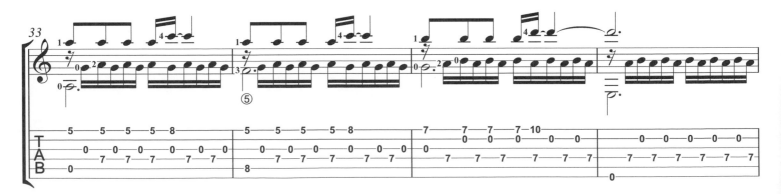

14

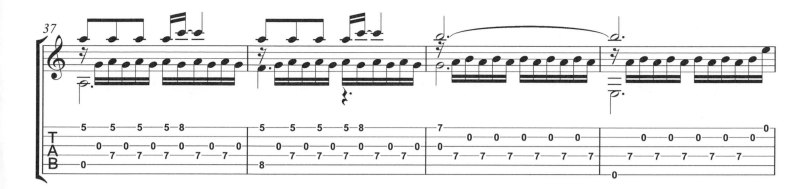

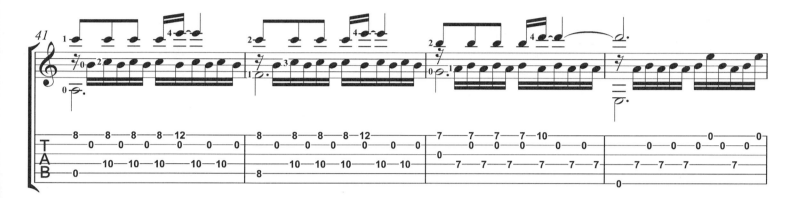

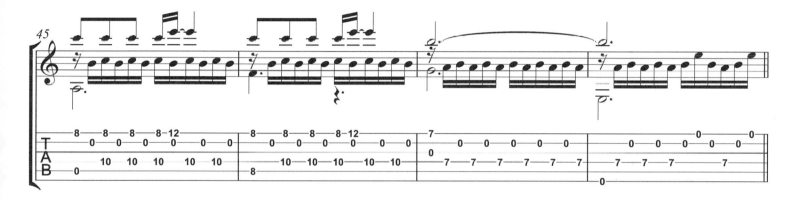

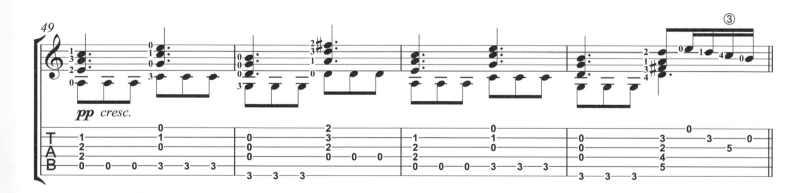

15

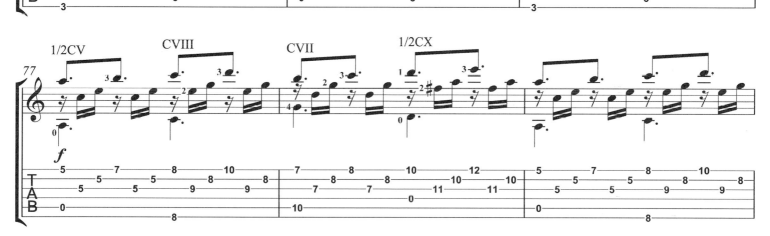

17

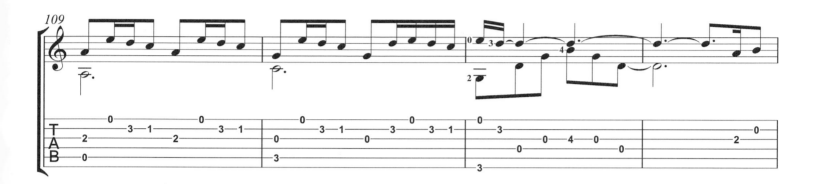

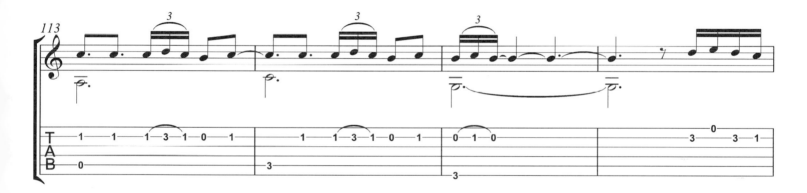

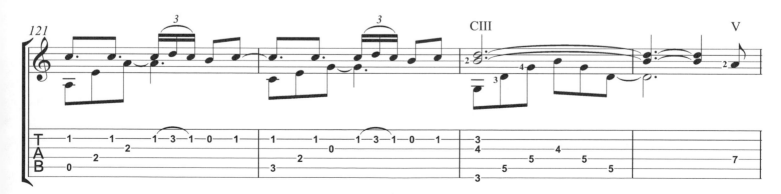

19

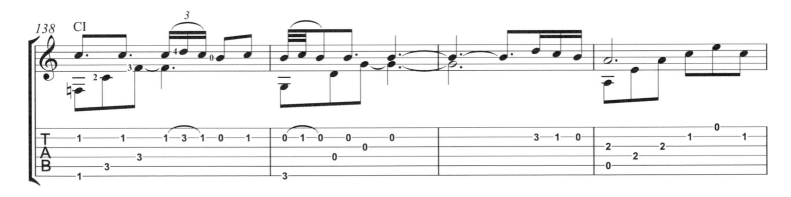

21

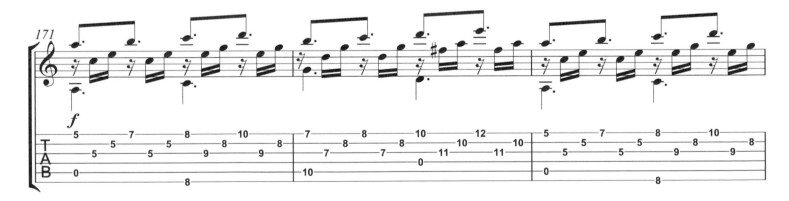

22

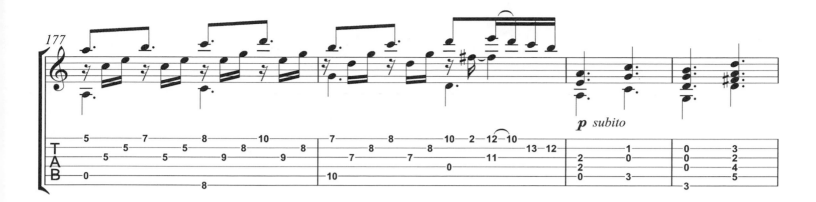

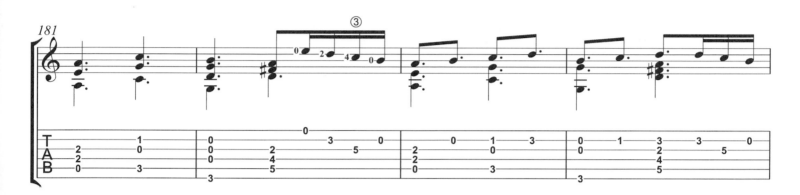

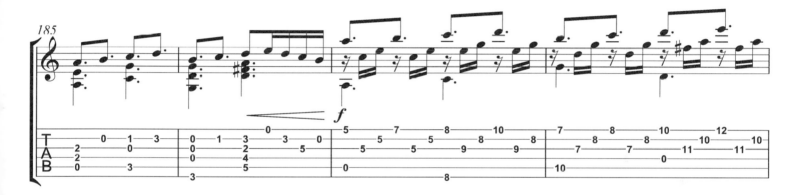

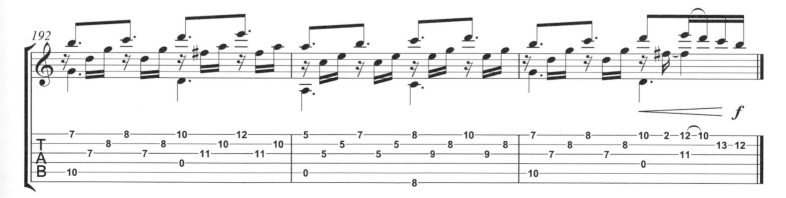

EDEN ROC

MUSIC BY LUDOVICO EINAUDI

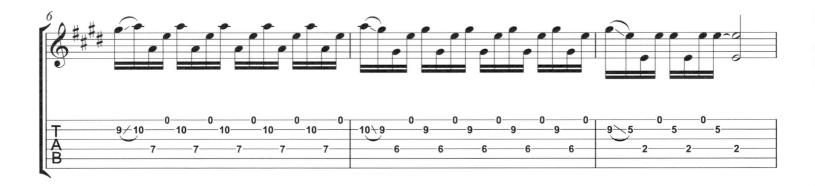

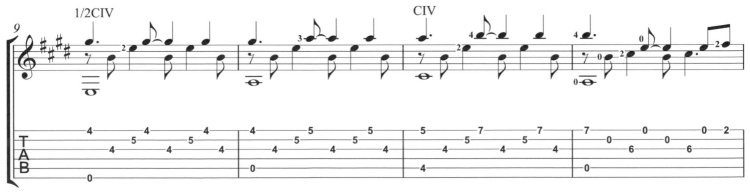

CII

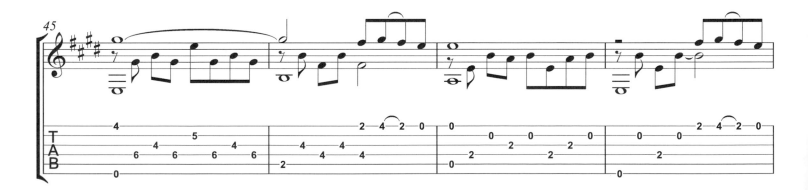

26

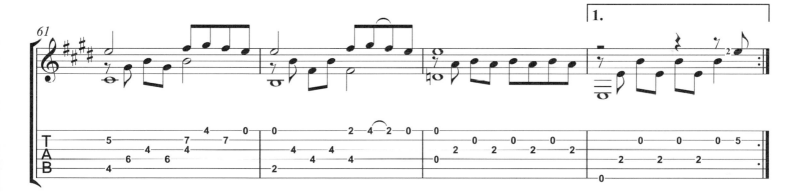

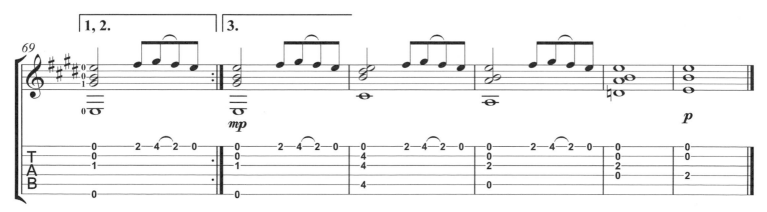

27

FAREWELL TO THE PAST

MUSIC BY LUDOVICO EINAUDI

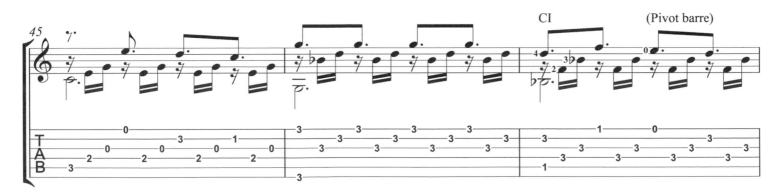

30

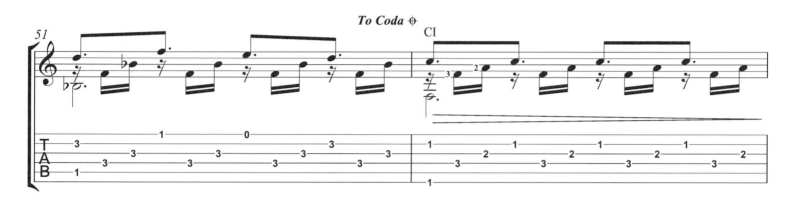

FUORI DALLA NOTTE

MUSIC BY LUDOVICO EINAUDI

Andante con moto

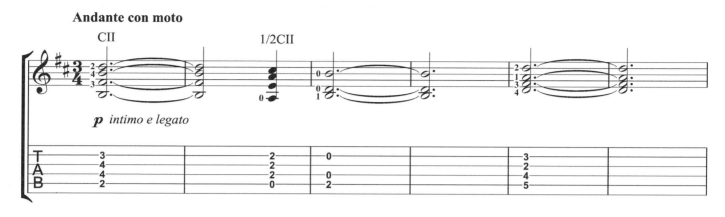

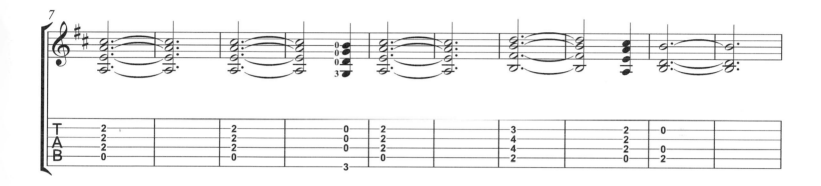

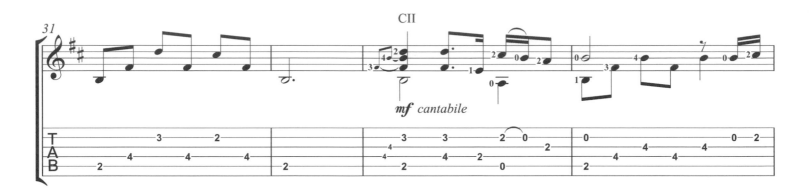

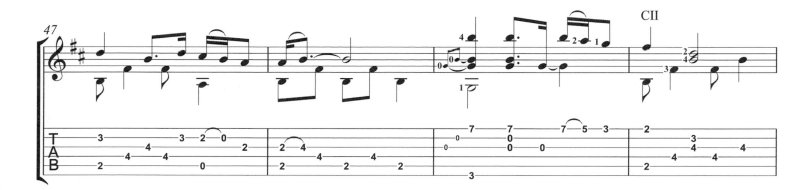

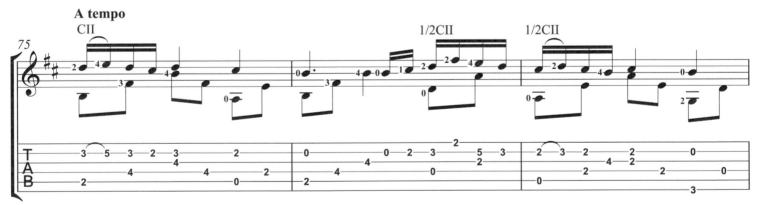

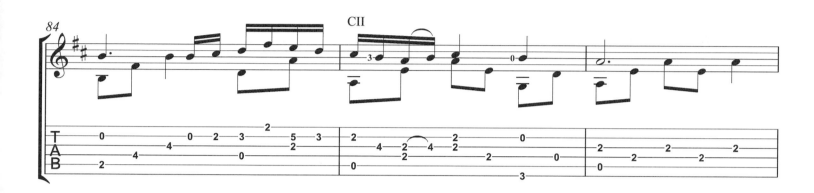

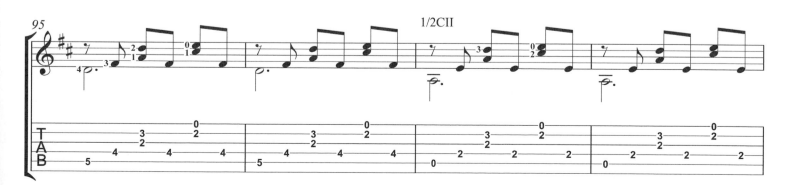

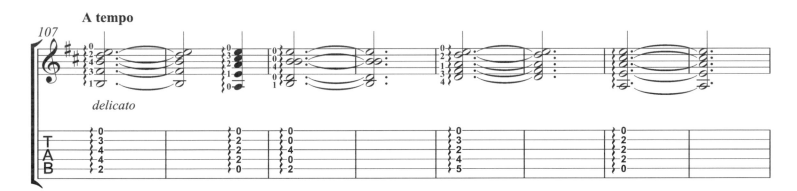

A tempo

delicato

un poco flessibile

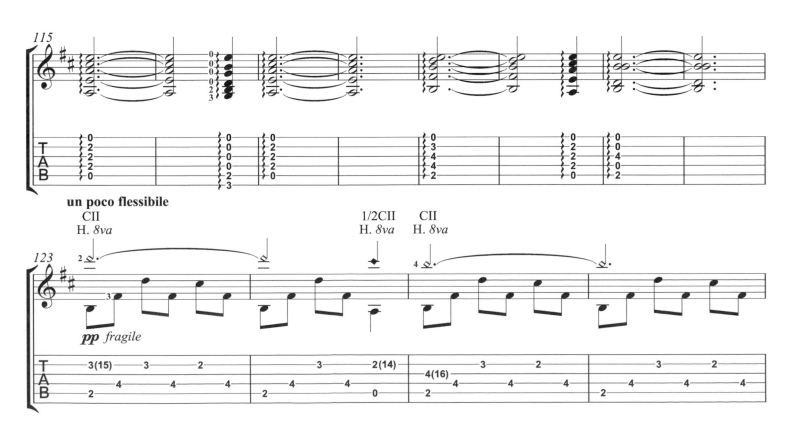

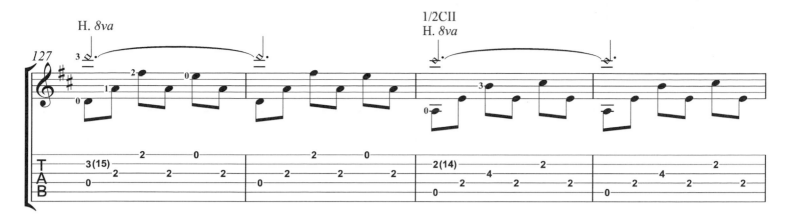

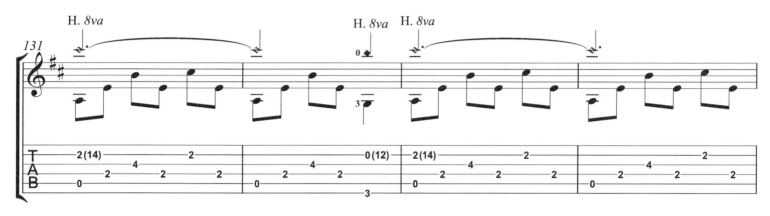

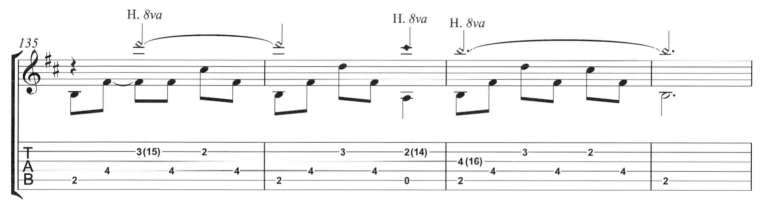

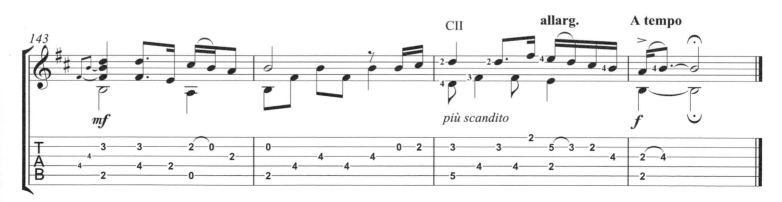

INDACO

MUSIC BY LUDOVICO EINAUDI

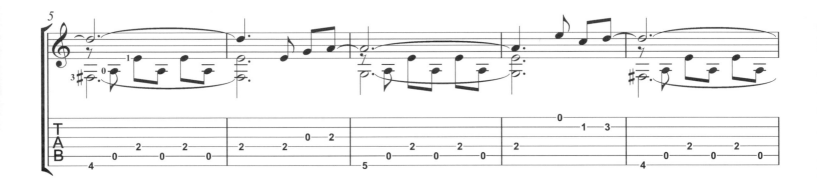

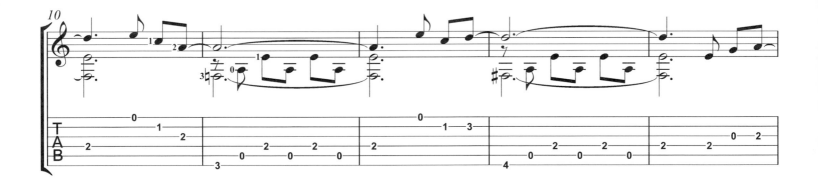

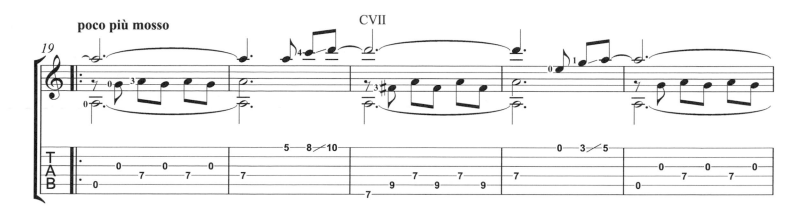

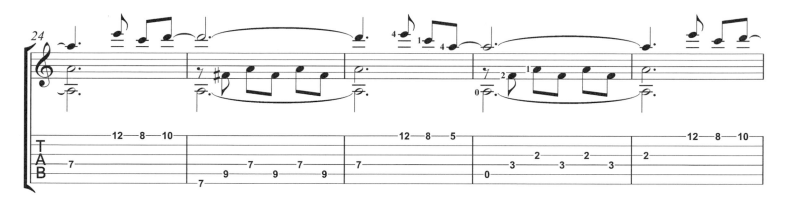

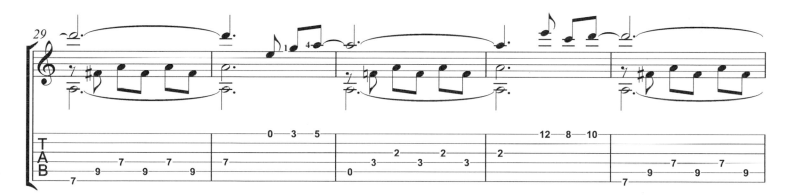

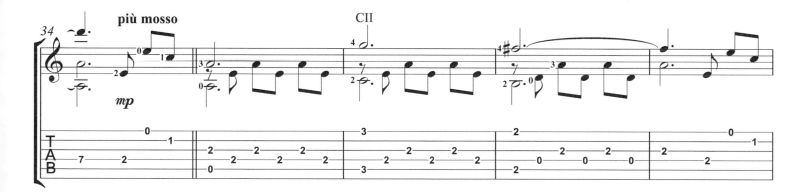

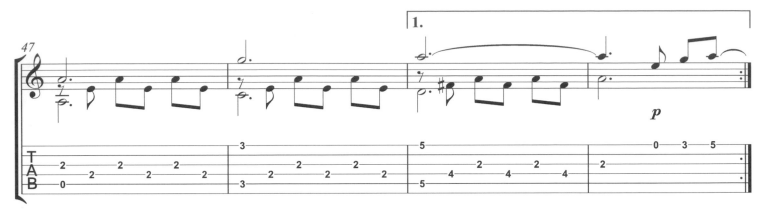

43

44

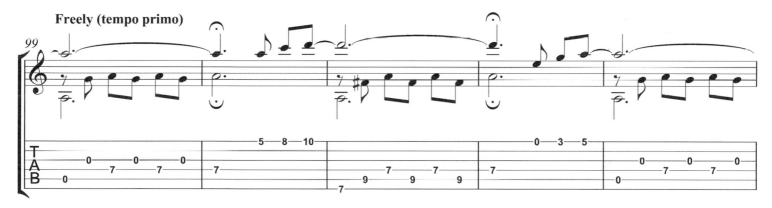

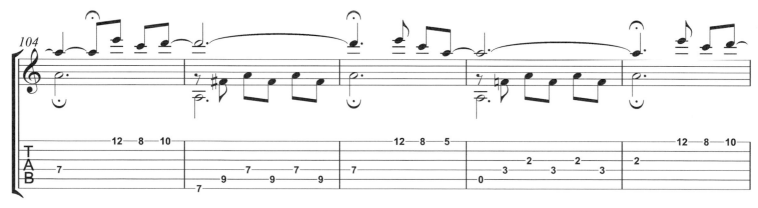

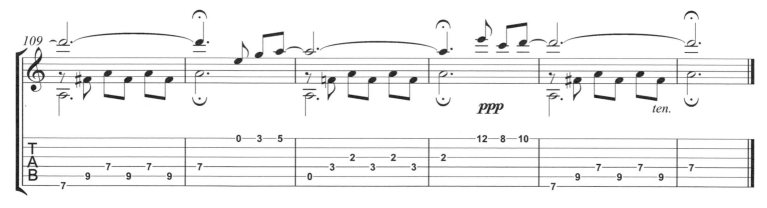

I GIORNI

MUSIC BY LUDOVICO EINAUDI

Andante

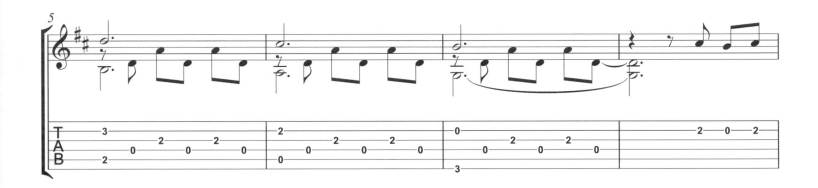

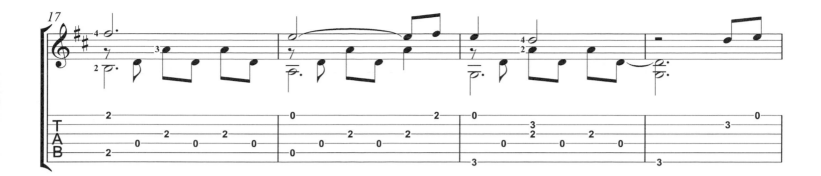

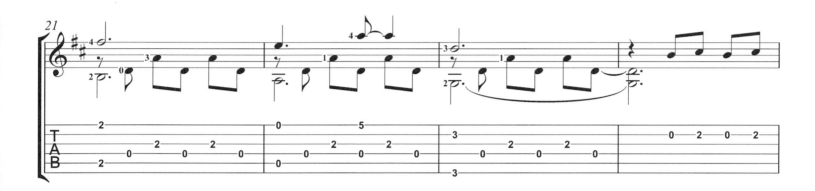

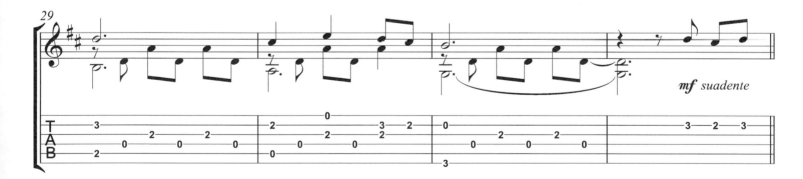

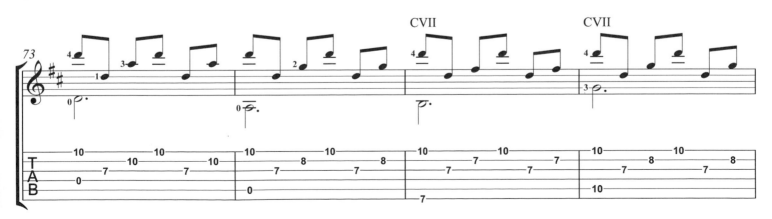

49

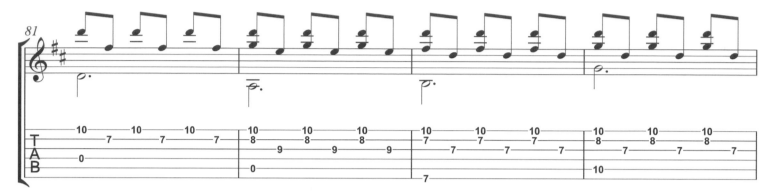

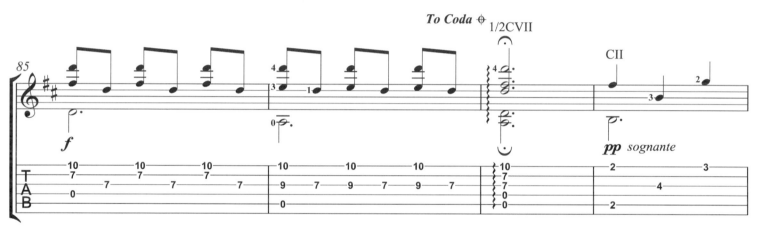

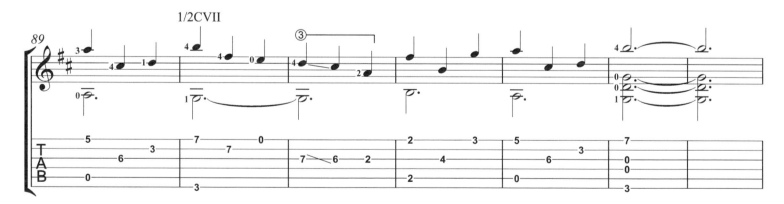

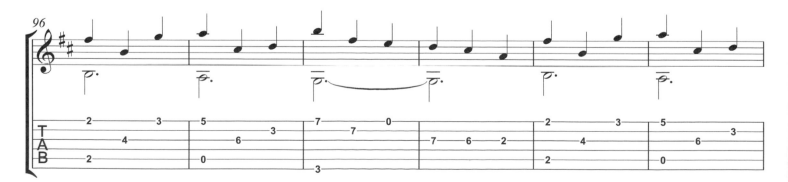

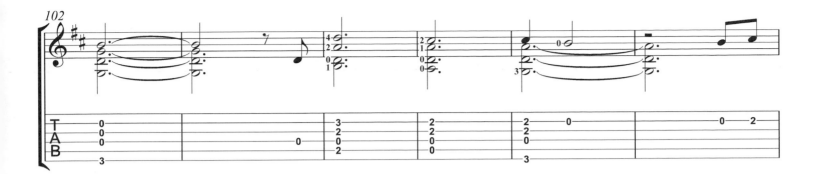

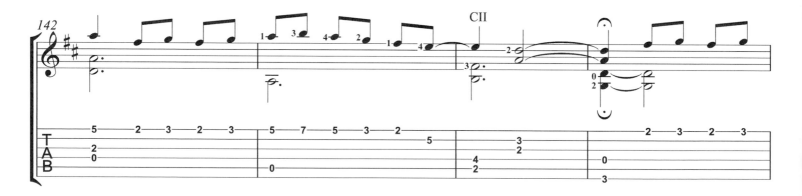

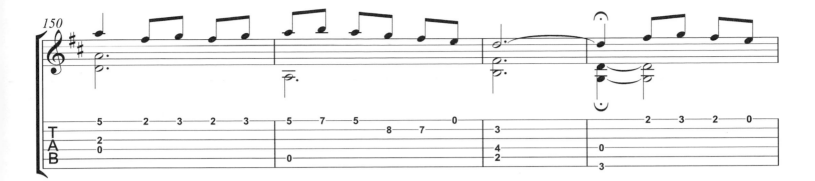

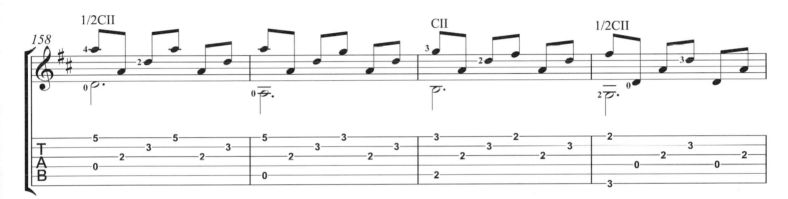

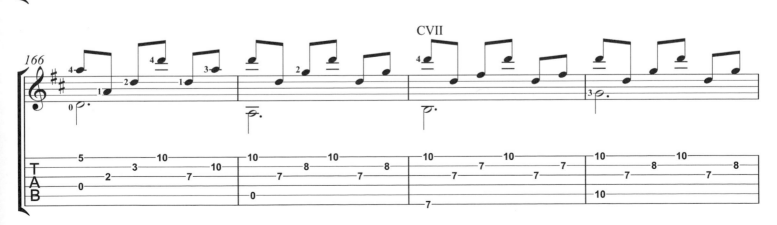

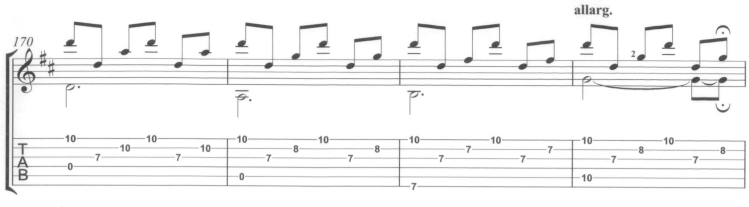

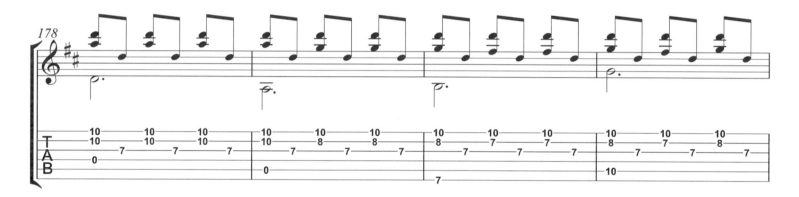

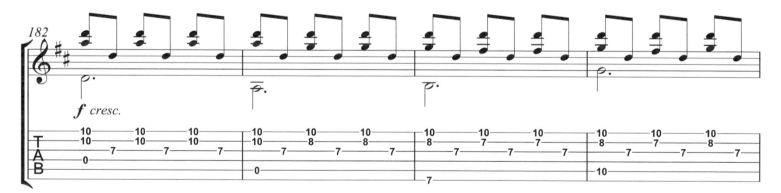

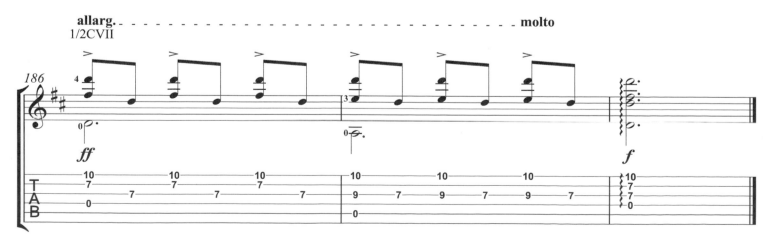

PRIMAVERA

MUSIC BY LUDOVICO EINAUDI

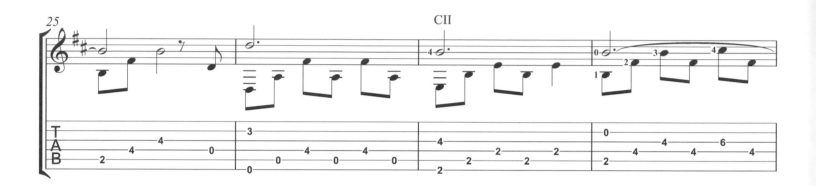

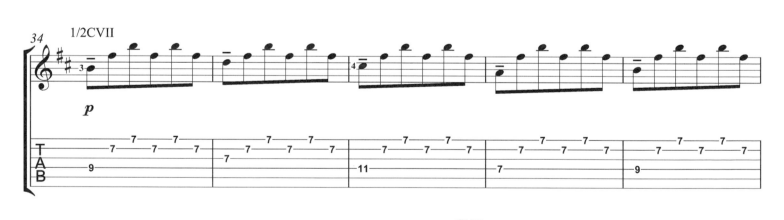

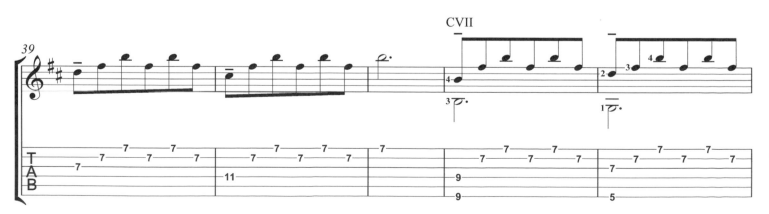

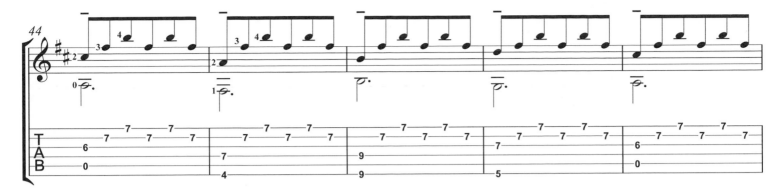

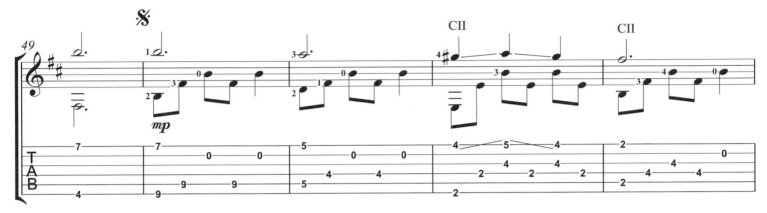

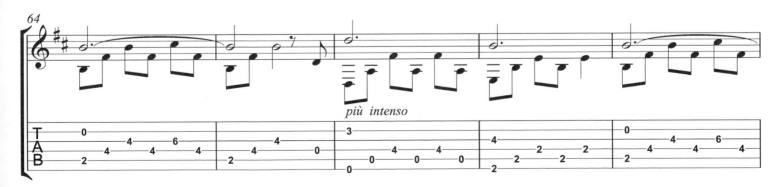

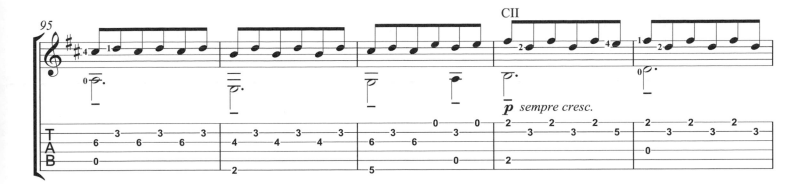

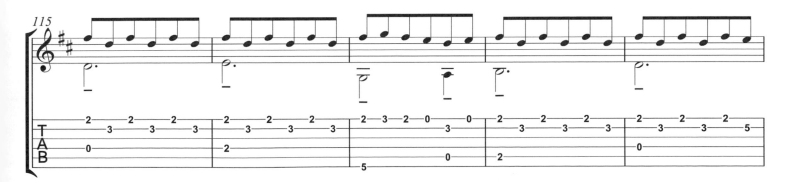

To Coda ⊕

D.S. al Coda
(with repeat)

⊕ *Coda*
rall.

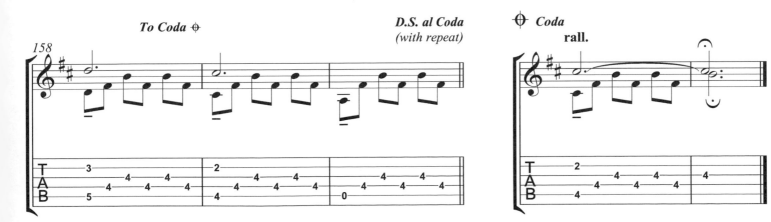

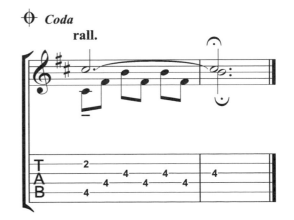

LE ONDE

MUSIC BY LUDOVICO EINAUDI

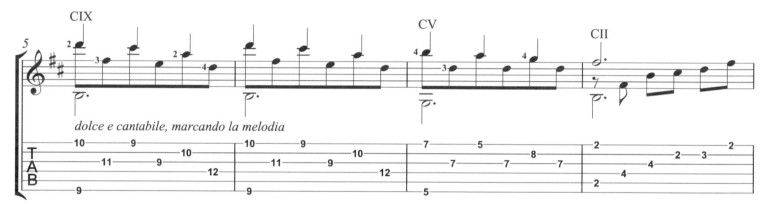

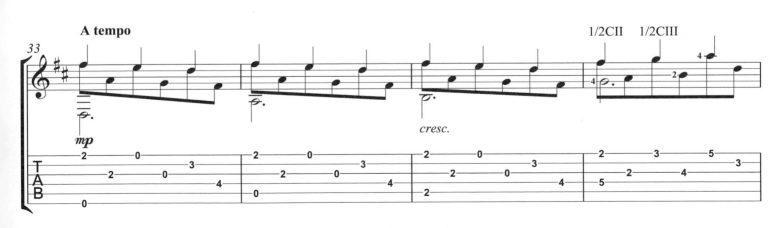

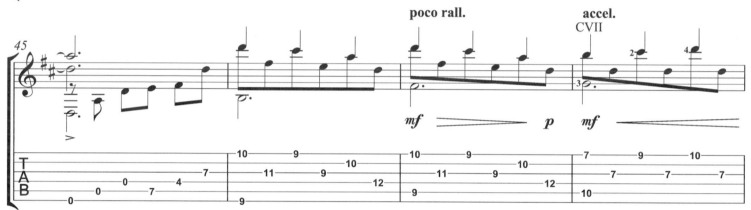

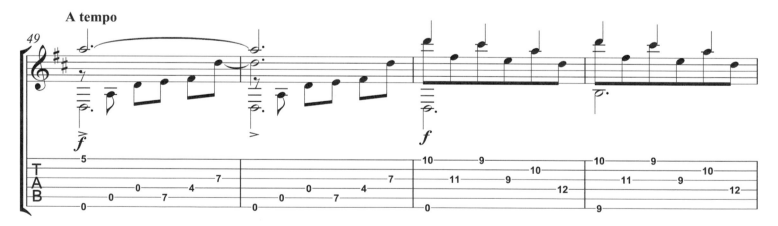

64

allarg.   A tempo

poco tratt.

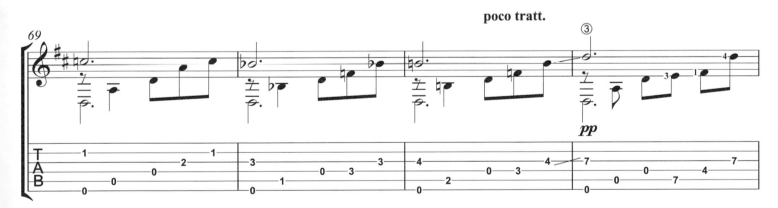

poco allarg.   A tempo

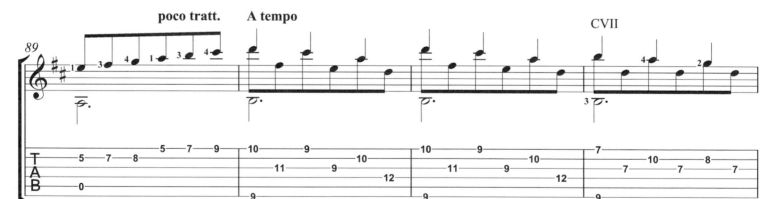

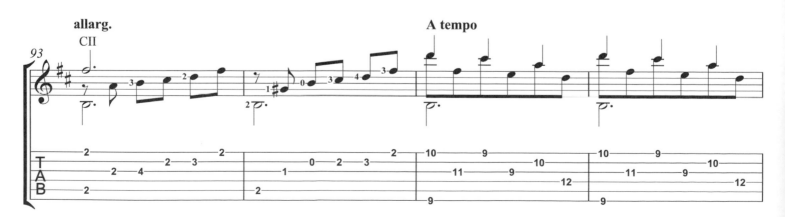

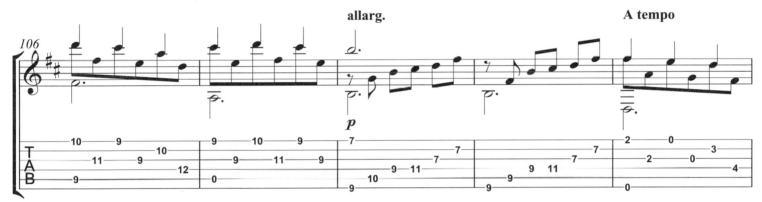

A tempo

rit.   accel.   A tempo

CVII

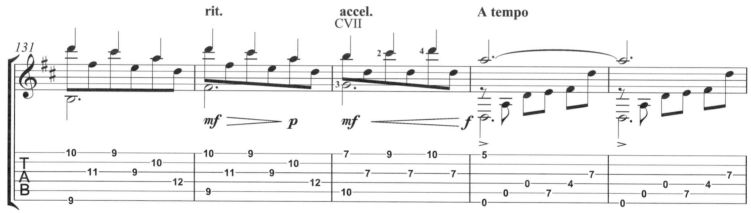

1/2CII

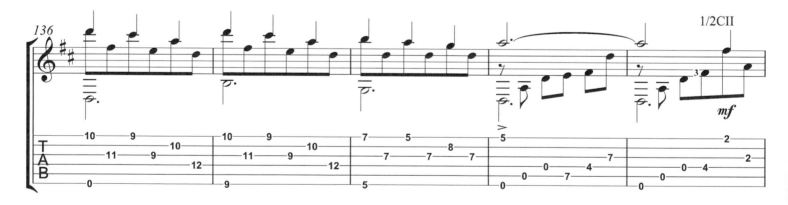

CII   (Pivot barre)

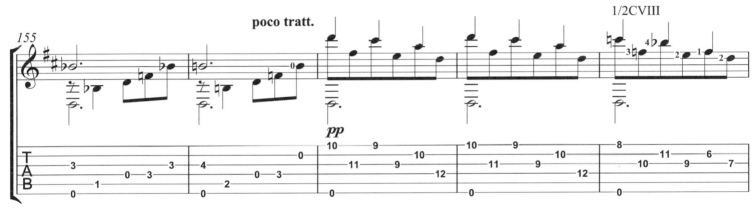

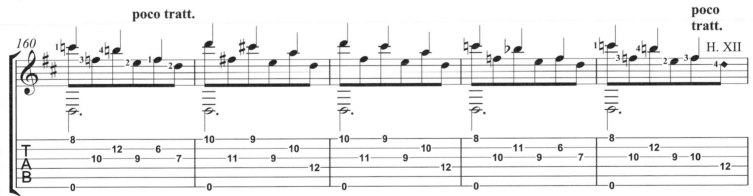

RESTA CON ME

MUSIC BY LUDOVICO EINAUDI

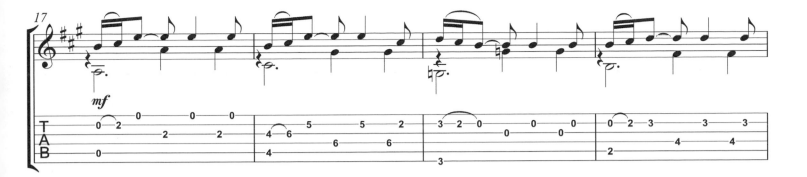

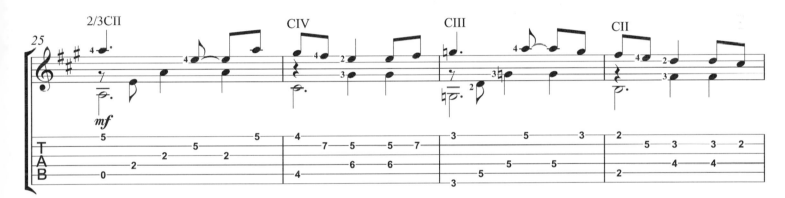

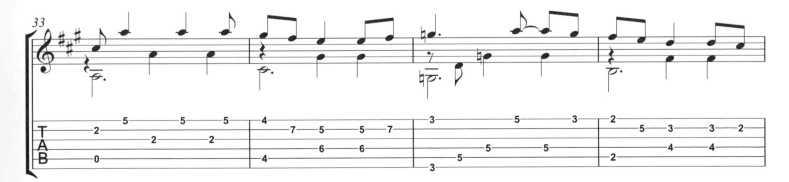

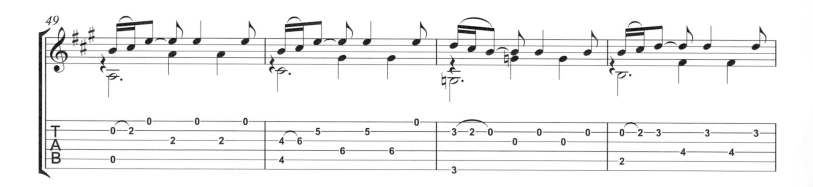

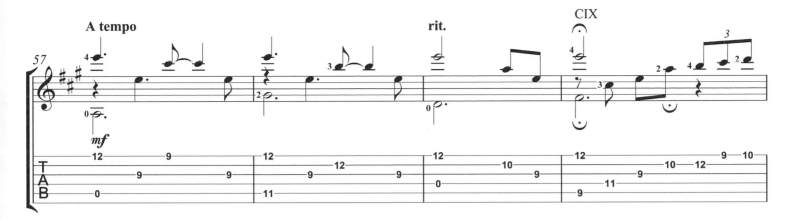

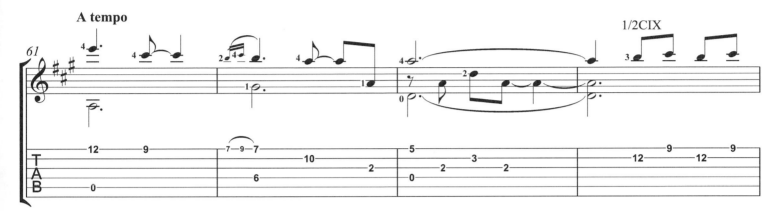

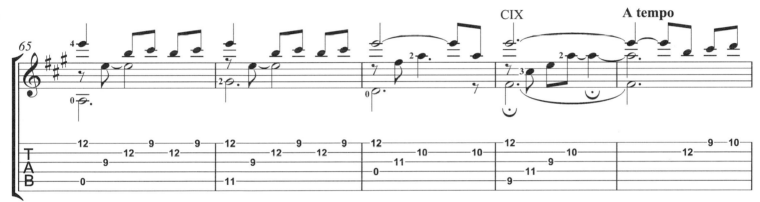

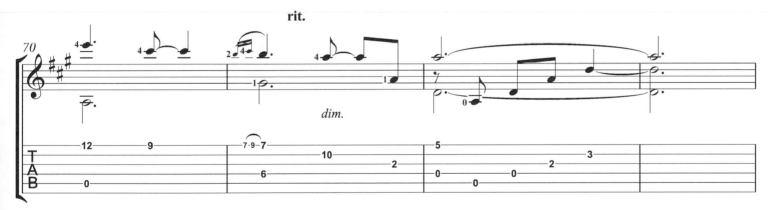

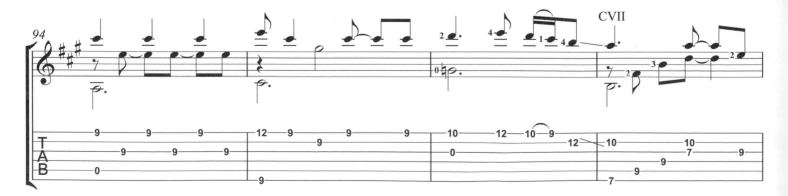

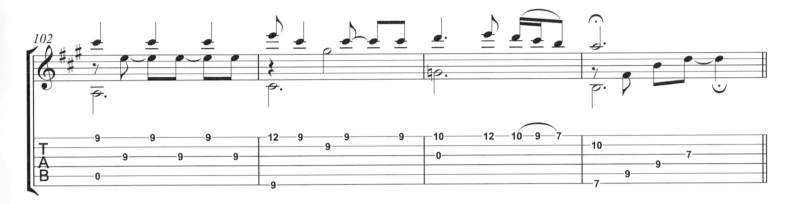

A tempo

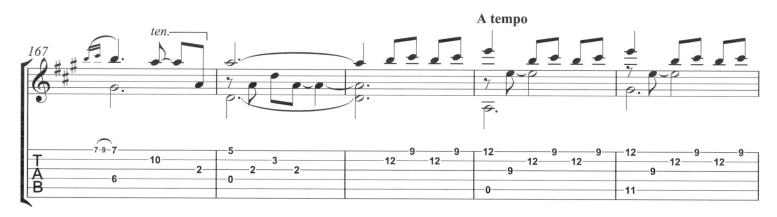

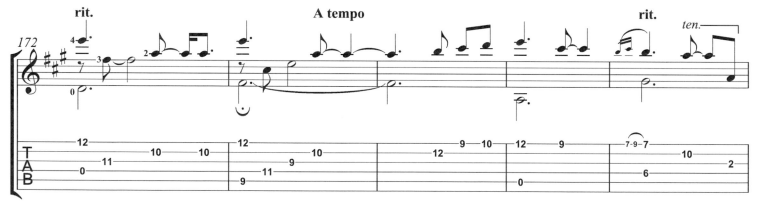

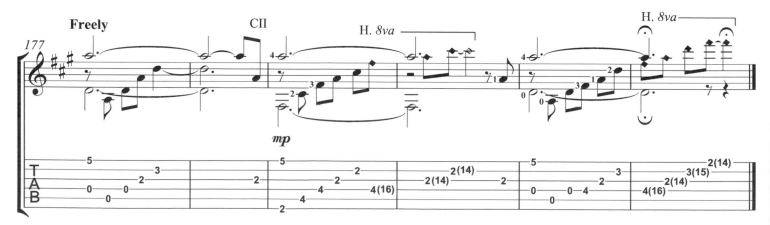

RÊVERIE

MUSIC BY LUDOVICO EINAUDI

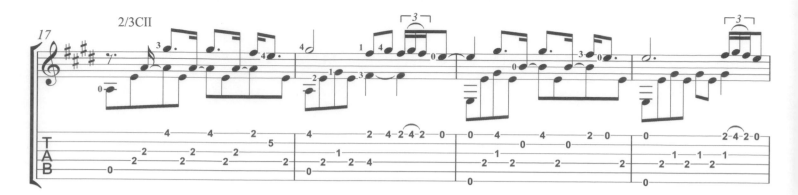

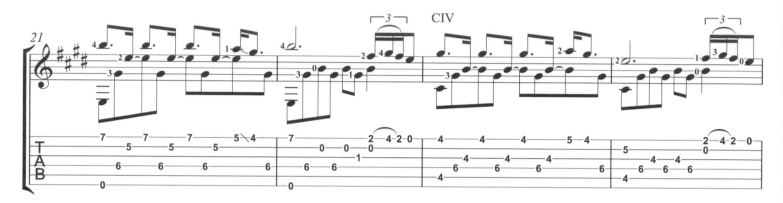

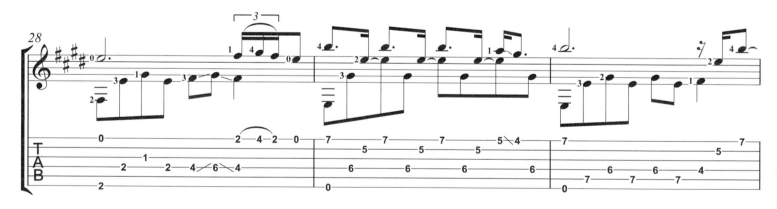

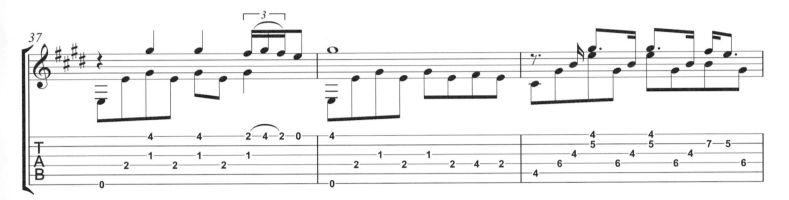

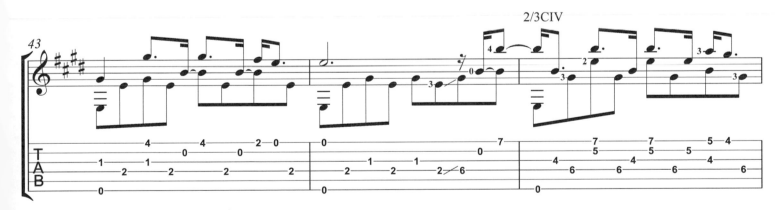

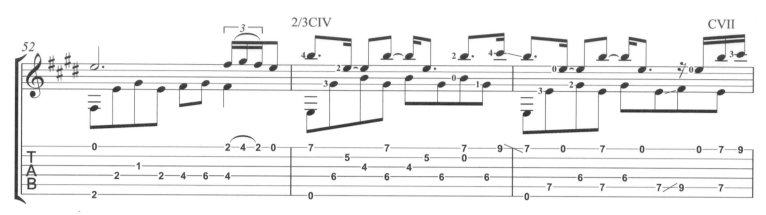

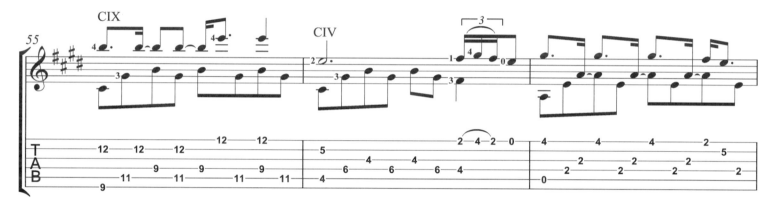

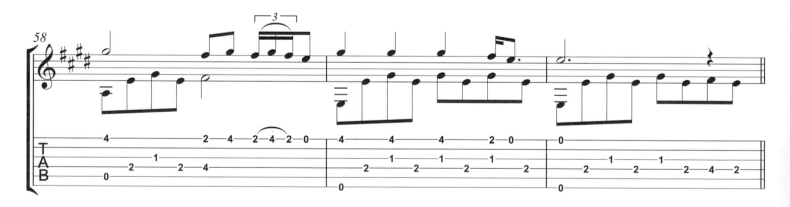

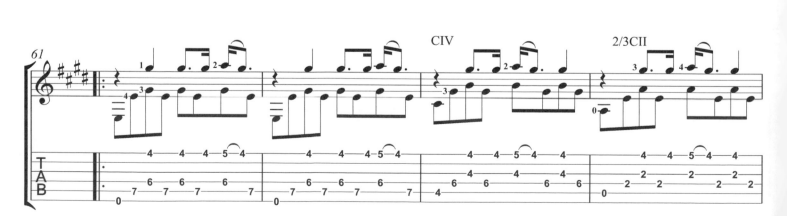

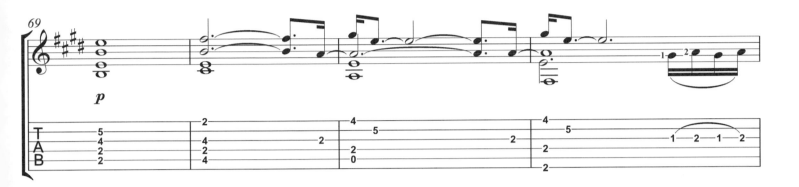

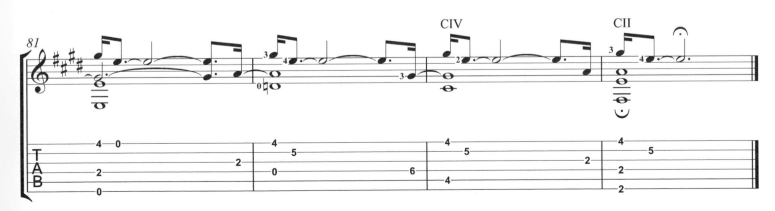

83

RITORNO

MUSIC BY LUDOVICO EINAUDI

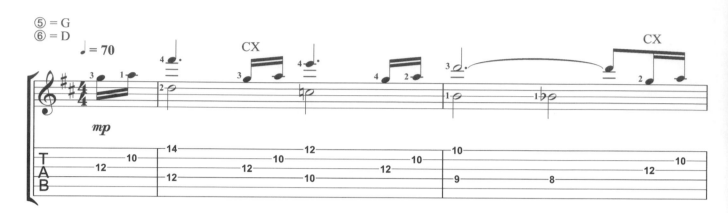

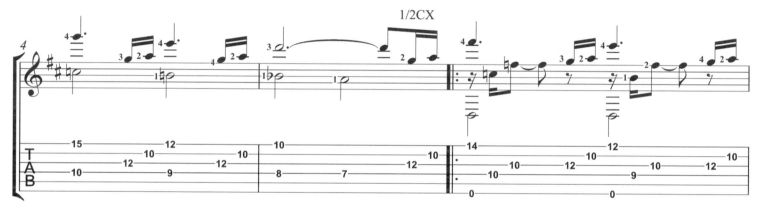

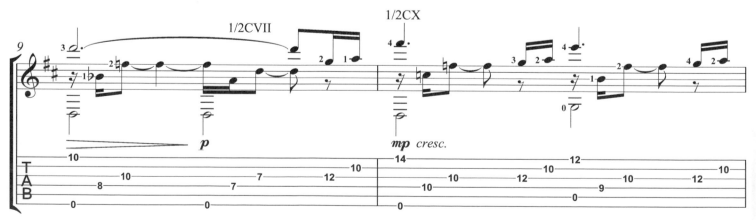

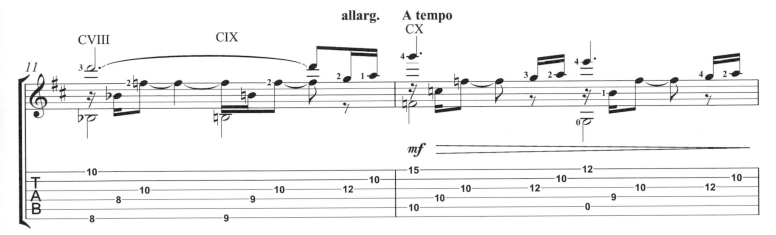

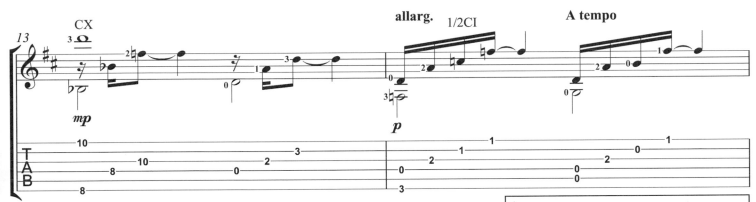

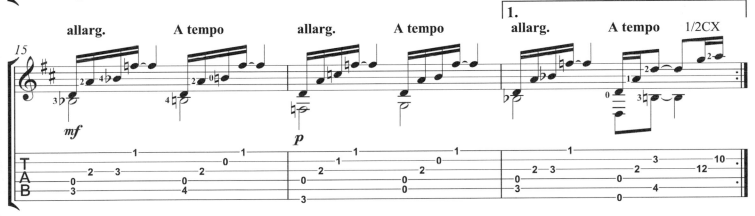

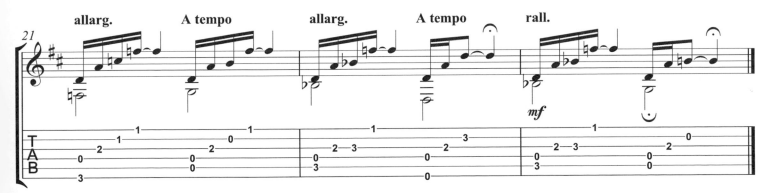

UNA MATTINA

MUSIC BY LUDOVICO EINAUDI

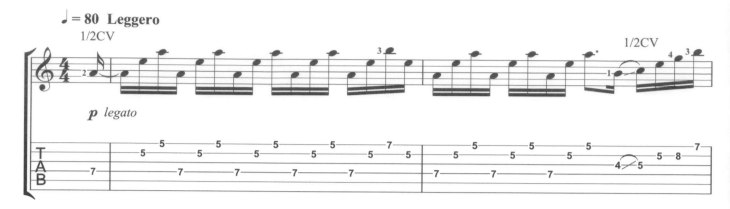

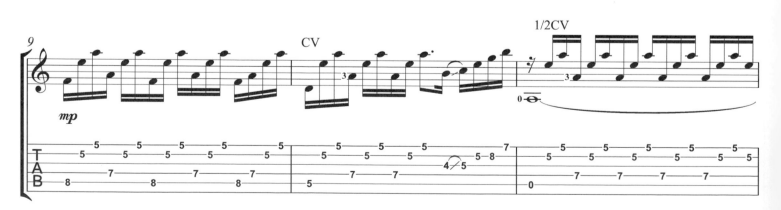

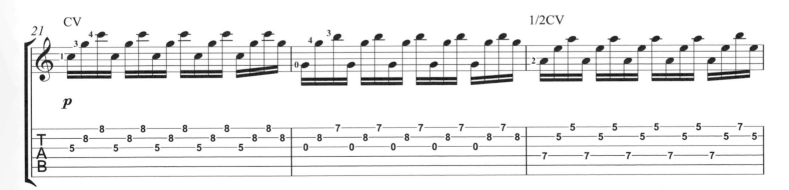

87

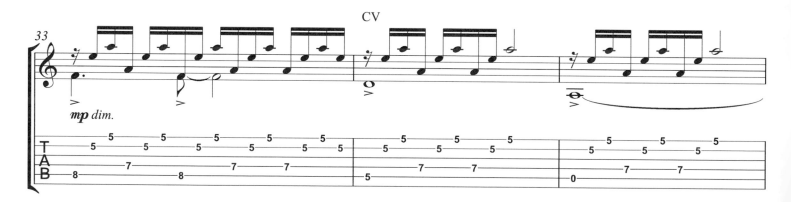

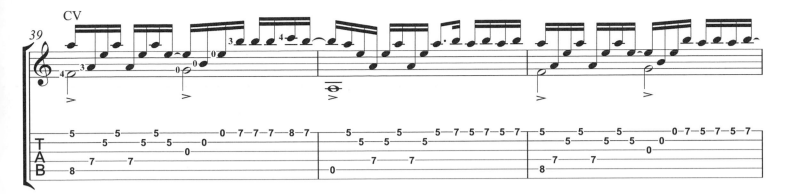

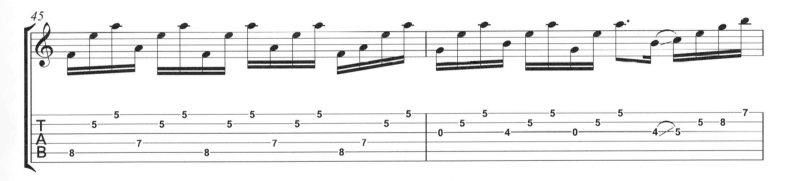

THE CRANE DANCE

MUSIC BY LUDOVICO EINAUDI

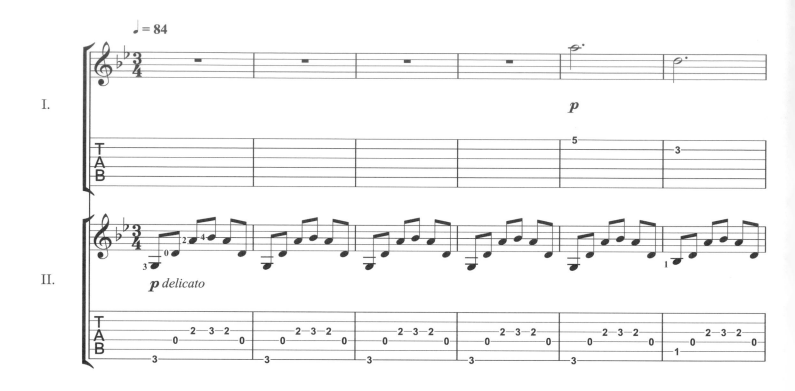

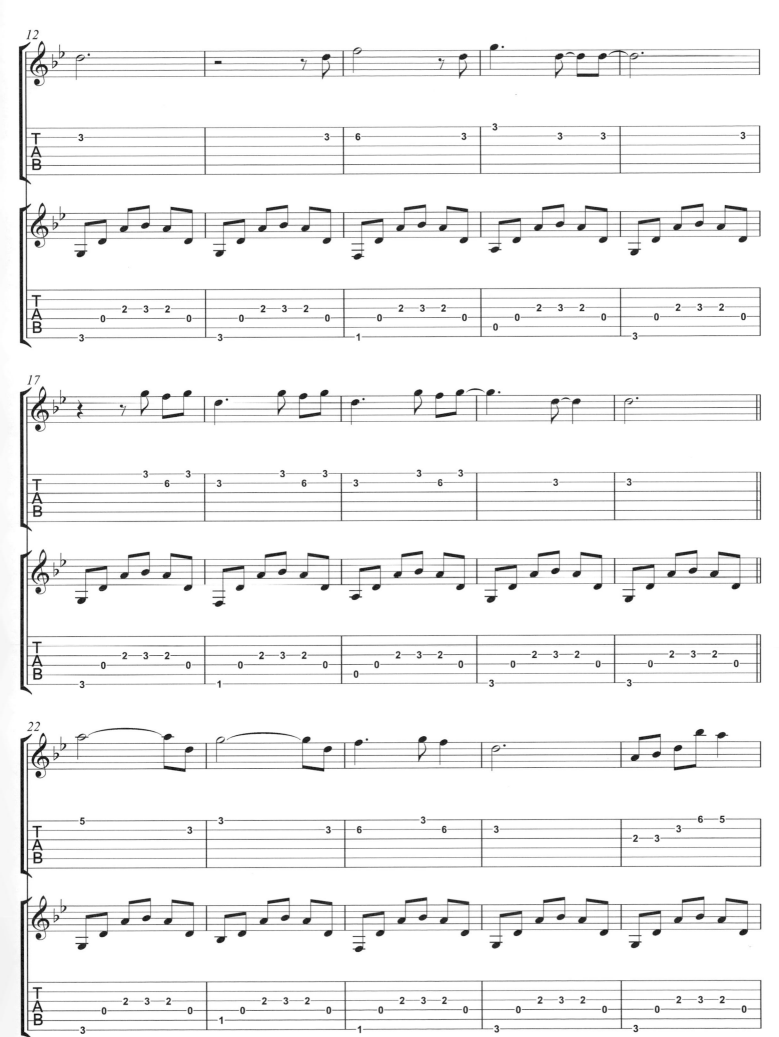

91

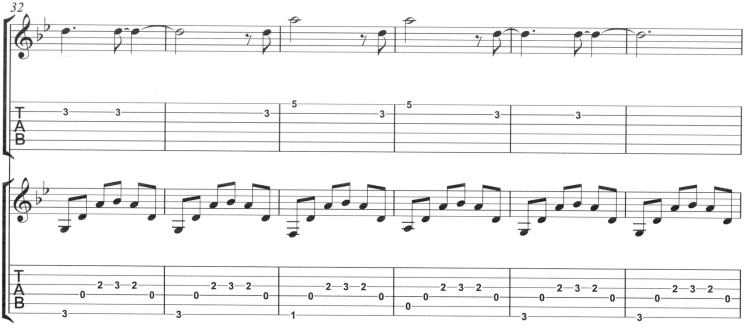

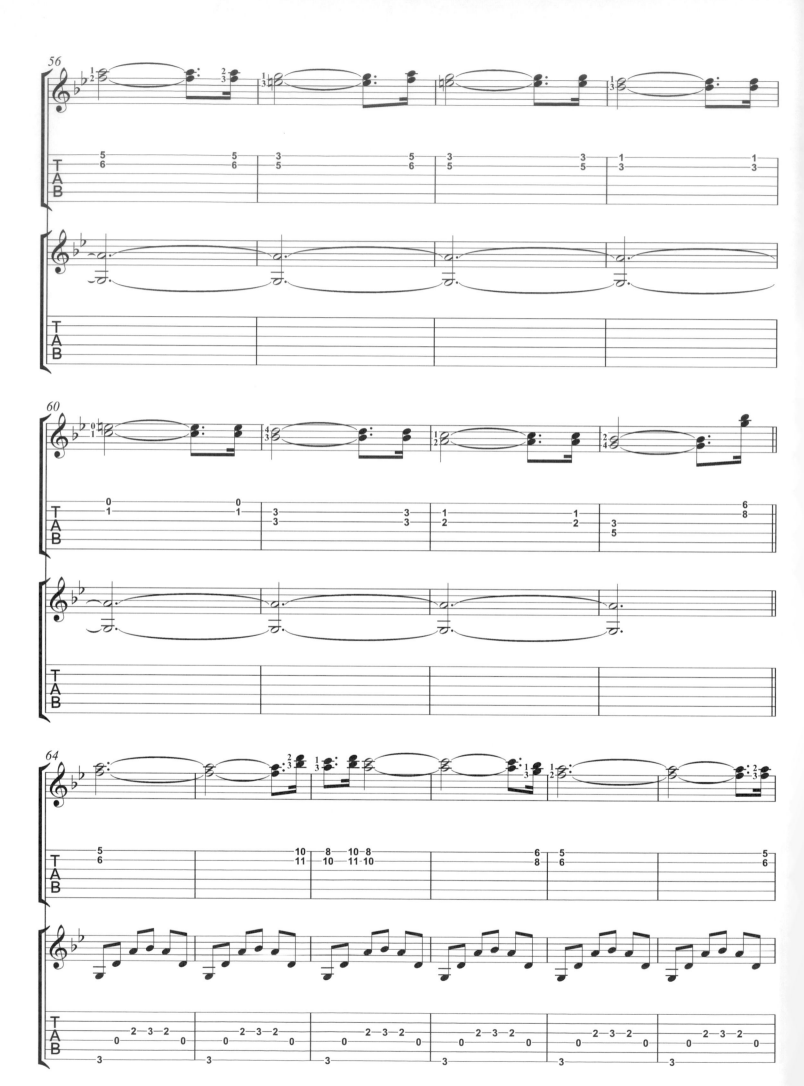

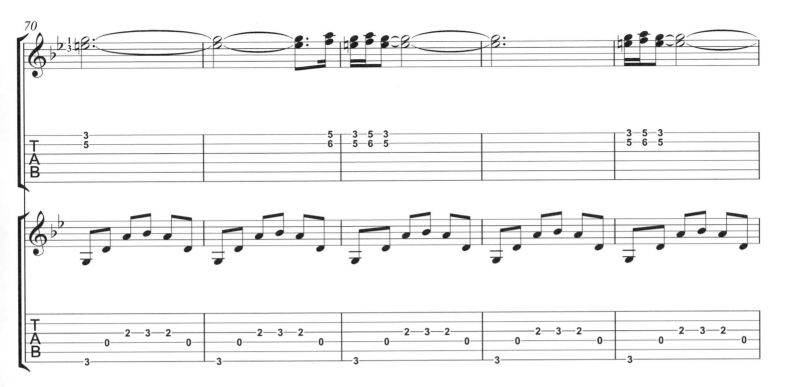